Baking in Wales

A group photograph of founder's family outside Derwen Bakery on its original site in 12 Thespian Street, Aberystwyth, Dyfed, c. 1918. Mrs. Mary Elizabeth Moore (nee Jenkins, extreme right) was one of the two sisters who ran the bakery at that date

Baking in Wales

S. MINWEL TIBBOTT

Assistant Keeper, Department of Buildings
and Domestic Life, Welsh Folk Museum

AMGUEDDFA GENEDLAETHOL CYMRU
NATIONAL MUSEUM OF WALES
CARDIFF, 1991

First published in 1991
© National Museum of Wales, Cardiff

Production: Hywel G. Rees
Design: Pica, Cardiff
Typesetting: Afal, Cardiff
Type: Baskerville 10/11 pt
Printing: Astec Press, Cardiff

ISBN 0 7200 0346 6

Front cover:
Derwen Bakery at the Welsh Folk Museum, St. Fagans, July 1990

Back cover:
A selection of breads and cakes baked at Derwen Bakery, Welsh Folk Museum, St. Fagans, July 1990

Preface

Commercial bakers were comparative newcomers among both urban and rural traders in Wales in the late nineteenth and early twentieth centuries. The tradition of home baking persisted in most rural households well into the mid-decades of the twentieth century, but with the growth of the urban villages and both market and industrial towns, domestic baking facilities changed. In general, town houses were fitted with iron ovens attached to kitchen ranges, which were not regarded as 'good bakers of bread'.

On settling in an urban area at the turn of the century, some Welsh business entrepreneurs of rural origin soon became aware of the needs of the local housewives. In the first instance, these 'bakers' set-up business by building a large brick oven on their premises in order to offer a new service to potential customers. Housewives were invited to bring their home-prepared dough to the 'bakehouse' and pay the baker for his service.

Derwen Bakery was one of three such bakehouses which were built in the market town of Aberystwyth, Dyfed, in the early twentieth century. Known locally as 'communes' (after 'communal oven'), they were built in strategic locations to serve different communities within the town itself.

Derwen bakehouse was built in 1900 by Evan Jenkins as a small business concern for his two daughters. He bought a house, known as Derwen, in Thespian Street and built a bakehouse in the garden behind it. The family were of a rural background, with the original home being at Dolgamlyn Farm in Cwmrheidol, near Aberystwyth. The large woodlands around the farm were developed as a timber business for the three sons and, consequently, they were able to provide a regular supply of the fuel required for the daily firing of the oven. Faggots of some 6-10 feet in length of oak or ash were usually carried to the bakehouse in two small horse-drawn carts every Monday.

Evan Jenkins appointed his daughter Catherine Jane to be in charge of the bakery, but she was to be assisted by his other daughter Mary Elizabeth, who also ran Derwen House as a guest house throughout the summer months. The sisters' daily routine began at 6.00a.m., with the exception of Saturday and Sunday, and their work-day did not end until approximately 10.00 o'clock at night. The oven was fired initially at 6.00a.m. and again at 2.00p.m. to provide the customers with two separate daily baking sessions for bread and cakes. Customers would have prepared the dough in their own homes. Having placed it in baking tins they would cover and carry it carefully to the bakehouse in good time for the appropriate baking session. They would return to collect the loaves at a given time and pay the bakers for their service. Baking charges varied according to the size of the loaves, namely from ¼d. to 1d. a loaf. The bakehouse was particularly busy at Christmas when customers used it for baking cakes and poultry, and also at Easter time when cakes and buns were baked in large batches for chapel functions.

Derwen Bakehouse served the local community on the northern side of Aberystwyth for some twenty-four years. When Catherine Jane Evans died in 1924 the business was closed. The building was abandoned and neglected over the years, but in the early 1980s the contemporary owners of the premises re-discovered it behind their garden shed. By this date it had fallen into disrepair, the roof having collapsed and a brick wall had been built around it. Fortunately, Mr. and Mrs. Ray Rees contacted the Welsh Folk Museum and offered the building as a donation for re-erection at St Fagans. The building measured about 26' by 12' and was divided into two parts. The oven chamber measured 9'9" by 8', and was fitted with a 2' square hinged iron door. The remaining area was used as a work room and was originally equipped with two long tables and shelves suspended on the walls for storing baking tins.

The bakehouse was re-erected on its new site at the Welsh Folk Museum during 1986-87. As much of the original material as possible was used and similar bricks and roofing slates were located to complete the building.

It was re-opened as a functional bakery in July 1987 when the resident bakers, Chris and Syd Aston fired the oven for the first time since 1924. Baking bread in a traditional timber-fired brick oven and making it available to visitors for purchasing was an innovation in the history of the Folk Museum. For the first time visitors were able to observe the bakers at work using traditional wooden appliances, mixing the dough by hand and managing the large brick oven in the traditional way. Loaves of bread and cakes soon proved popular and were readily purchased day after day. From then on the bakery has been well established and is now one of the major attractions at the Museum.

The aim of this booklet is to outline the development of baking in the home, primarily looking at the Welsh housewife's skill of preparing and baking flat breads on the bakestone, discussing the art of mixing and moulding leavened dough and tracing the history of its baking from the pot-oven method to the built-in wall oven. Commercial baking in the developing towns of the nineteenth century is also mentioned. Documentary evidence has been corroborated by oral testimony and excerpts from recorded interviews with experienced housewives and bakers are quoted in the text as illustrations.

Traditional Breads of Wales

'They eat meat in abundance, but very little bread'

Traditional descriptions of early Welsh diet and economy are based to a large extent on statements made by that shrewd observer, Gerallt Gymro *(Giraldus Cambrensis)*. When journeying through Wales with Archbishop Baldwin in 1188, he placed on record in *Description of Wales* his view of the Welsh character and his impressions of Welsh society. The economic basis of this society was the pasturing of flocks and herds. 'Most of their lands', he said, 'serves for grazing, little of it is used for tillage, still less for gardens and scarcely any for orchards'. He noted that most of the people lived on the produce of their herds, with milk, butter, cheese and oats being staple articles in their diet. He added '. . . they eat meat in abundance, but very little bread'.

However, his statement that the Welsh ate little bread, or did very little ploughing except in March or April for the sowing of oats, can be counter-balanced by other evidence which reveals the basic importance of bread and of tillage. Indeed the detailed attention given to the ox and the ploughman in the Laws of Hywel Dda, for instance, emphasises the importance of tillage even in pre-Norman times. Mr. Ffransis G. Payne in his book *Yr Aradr Gymreig,* (The Welsh Plough) has supplied ample evidence of Welsh tillage and its social implications from the tenth to the fifteenth centuries.

The Laws of Hywel Dda codified in the eleventh century provide sound evidence of the growing of wheat, barley and oats as main crops, and both wheatbread and oatbread are specified as part of the food-tithe paid to the king by bondmen and freemen alike. Included in a winter's food-tithe were 'sixty loaves of wheaten bread if wheat is grown . . . if not, let the bread be oaten'. Archaeological excavations at Dinas Powys, Dinas Emrys and Pant-y-saer, Glamorgan, have all produced hand-mills for grinding flour. This evidence again shows the importance of cereal crops despite Gerallt's assertions to the contrary. It is reasonable to conclude that this early Welsh economy was based on mixed farming, more or less adapted to local conditions of soil, altitude and climate. This economy sufficed to provide the people with a subsistence diet based mainly on meat, dairy produce and oatbread. Gerallt Gymro described the Welsh as not being addicted to gluttony, but dedicating their whole day to work and in the evening partaking of a moderate meal. Guests were welcome and a meal would be prepared according to the number and dignity of the persons assembled and to the wealth of the family who entertained.

'The kitchen did not supply many dishes nor high seasoned incitements to eating: the home is not adorned with tables, cloths and napkins, they study nature more than splendour for which reason they place all the dishes together upon rush mats and on large platters, around which the guests sit in threes and not in pairs as in other countries. They also serve the food on large thin cakes, baked daily'.

Despite a more systematic approach to land cultivation following the Tudor enclosures, and with the growing of crops for home consumption established on a firmer footing, farming in Wales still remained predominantly pastoral. Meat was eaten regularly, and the bread was made of oats or rye.

Writing during the reign of Elizabeth I, the Pembrokeshire historian, George Owen of Henllys, described the diet of the poorest husbandman in his county thus:

'the common foode is beefe, mutton, pigge, goose, lambe, veale and kydd . . .'

He also notes that they persisted in growing oats, as did their fathers in previous centuries, on land suitable for producing wheat or rye; they preferred *yr hen rawn* (the old cereal).

The prominence of oats, and to a lesser extent of barley, in the diet of the people of rural Wales in the eighteenth century has been noted by visitors to the country, and this evidence has been corroborated by eminent historians. Thomas Pennant in *Tours in Wales,* describing the welcome he received at the home of the landowner, Evan Lloyd of Cwm Bychan, near Harlech, in 1799 writes

'He welcomed us with ale and potent beer, to wash down coch yr wden *or hung goat, and the cheese compounded of the milk of cow and sheep . . . The mansion is a true specimen of an ancient seat of a gentleman of Wales. The furniture rude, the most remarkable are the* cistiau styffylog *[or the oatmeal chests] which held the essential part of the provision of the Welsh people in the eighteenth century.'*

Our forefathers' staff of life at that time was oats, and the general sustenance of the ordinary farmer in Wales during that century was barley bread, oatmeal, *llymru*, *cawl* (broth) and a little bacon. Another author, William Williams of Llandygai, Caernarfonshire, (Gwynedd) dealing with the same period, gives specification of the food of the people living in that part of the country.

'. . in farmhouses they have three sorts of bread, namely wheat, barley and oatmeal, but the oatmeal they chiefly use: this with butter, cheese and potatoes is their common summer food'.

When Benjamin Heath Malkin visited Glamorgan in 1803 he drew attention to the types of bread eaten in different parts of the county

'I have already mentioned that in the vale all eat good wheaten bread, in the mountains, some oaten bread is used but not so generally as in former times. In Gower, they eat barley bread for the most part'.

In his book *A General view of Agriculture and Domestic Economy . . .* (1810), Walter Davies criticises the continued reluctance among the Welsh farming community to grow wheat.

'Thousands of persons who seldom eat any other bread than that of oats and barley, have thousands of acres under their management capable of bearing plentiful crops of wheat but are so accustomed to oatbread that they seem pre-possessed with the idea of the impracticability of growing that superior grain'.

However, wheaten bread has not been so important an element in the national diet of Wales as of many other countries and it was not generally eaten at the table of ordinary Welsh folk until the later decades of the nineteenth century. The dramatic fall in the price of wheat in the 1880s led to the decline in the eating of oat and barley bread.

Another valuable source of information regarding the foods of the Welsh people during the latter part of the nineteenth and the early decades of the twentieth century is that gained from oral testimony. Details of the preparation and cooking of everyday foods have been handed down orally from mother to daughter, from generation to generation. Evidence, gathered widely from informants in different areas, has revealed that the general sustenance foods of the farming community in Wales at the turn of the century were based on home-cured salt meat, home grown vegetables, dairy products and by-products, and the main cereal crops, namely oats and barley. The types of bread eaten varied slightly from area to area; it was the general custom to buy imported flour which was added to the home produced wheat or barley meal to give a better quality mixed bread *(bara cymysg)*. Barley bread of inferior quality, however, was still baked for the menservants in some districts. In the hilly regions where oats was the only cereal crop grown the inhabitants would buy all the required flour to make refined bread. However, oatcakes continued to be baked, but now were regarded as being supplementary to the home-baked white bread.

Flat Breads and the Bakestone Method

The most primitive method of baking bread was to place small rounds of unleavened dough in warm embers on hot stones or a pre-heated hearth stone and allow to bake until they became hard. Examples of hearthcakes found at the first century BC lake village of Glastonbury survive and were found in the form of very hard small buns. On analysis it was established that they were made of fragments of whole grains of wheat, hulled barley, wild oat, chess and a seed of common oracle. There were no traces of leaven. The traditional flat-bread of Wales, oatcake, our forefathers' staff of life since the Middle Ages, was baked by a similar but slightly more sophisticated method and it continued to be a living tradition well into the twentieth century.

The logical development from the primitive method of baking on a hot hearth or flagstone was the use of a thin slab built into and projecting from a wall, sufficiently high to allow for a fire on the ground below, as was found on the site of a Romano-British village in Staffordshire. A similar 'baking stone' was found on the yard of a farm near Llanwrtyd, Breconshire (Powys), measuring twelve inches long and ten inches wide. The portable, circular baking stone, is part of this earlier tradition and it continued to be in use well into the nineteenth century. Circular iron plates were also introduced in the medieval period and were employed for baking. The Welsh noun *gradell* (griddle) appears in the Laws of Hywel Dda and is included among the iron objects made by the blacksmith.

Bakestones and iron planks are listed in seventeenth and early eighteenth century inventories of Welsh landed gentry, yeomen and small farmers alike. A careful inventory of goods in the kitchen at Plas Brondanw, Merioneth (Gwynedd) dated 11 April, 1713 includes three iron bakestones, while the inventory (1676) of goods in the possession of William Rowland, a small farmer of Llanfabon, Glamorgan, refers

Rolling out oatcakes: Mrs. Catrin Evans, Llanuwchllyn, Gwynedd

specifically to 'a tripod and one iron plate for baking oaten bread'. A similar reference, 'an iron plank for baking of bread' was found in the will (1729) of one William John, yeoman of Myddfai, Carmarthenshire (Dyfed). The reference to 'one backinstone' (value 1/-) in the inventory of goods belonging to a William Evan of Pencarreg, Carmarthenshire, is of particular significance.

When employed on a flat-hearth, the bakestone was supported by an iron tripod over the fire. In many areas, however, and more especially in south-west Wales, it was held in position on a circular iron frame with a half-loop handle suspended from a hook and chain. Other examples of bakestones were made with a half-hoop handle attached to them for suspension. With the introduction of the built-up iron grate or range, it became common practice to rest the bakestone on the two hobs on either side of the fireplace. Peat was recognised as one of the most suitable fuels for heating the bakestone, but coal, wood, furze, gorse and straw were also used according to local resources.

An accessory tool used in conjunction with the bakestone in Wales was a slender wooden spade or slice. Carved by the male members of the family, it was made specifically for turning the loaves and cakes when baked on the bakestone. The size and shape of the blade varied slightly from area to area, and a similar variation in the Welsh names by which it was known was also discerned. *Rhawlech,* with the variants *awlerch* and *owlerch,* was the general name given to it in Carmarthenshire and Cardiganshire, *sgleish* or *sleish* the equivalent used in Glamorgan and Breconshire, with the name *crafell* used throughout the counties of north Wales. *Crafell* was defined by Thomas Jones (1688) as a 'curry comb, also a wooden slice to turn oatcakes with'.

The bakestone was in constant use in most parts of the country well into the twentieth century. It was employed widely throughout the counties of north and south Wales, primarily for baking unleavened flat-breads, including oatbread, and at a later date, a variety of batter-type cakes.

Basically, the ingredients of oatmeal and water and sometimes a little fat, were mixed to form a dough which was finally baked on the bakestone. The art lay in the rolling-out of the dough to form large wafer-thin rounds with fine even edges. Two different methods of

Rolling out oatcakes

Rolling out oatcakes: Mrs. May Davies, Llan-saint, Dyfed

rolling-out were practised in Wales, the one confined to specific areas in south-west Wales and the other employed fairly generally throughout the counties of north Wales (see illustrations).

Baking the oatcakes followed a similar pattern throughout the country. The bakestone would be pre-heated to a certain temperature which the experienced housewife could easily gauge.

> 'Oh well, you'd brush it clean to start with, and take a pinch of oatmeal and spread it across the griddle. If it started to change colour, to turn yellow, it was ready. It was hot enough then'.

The large thin cake, equal in size to a large dinner plate with a fine even edge was then deftly placed on the bakestone (griddle). Removed from a pre-hardened batch on the table, it would be carried

11

Baking and drying oatcakes

Here the cakes were allowed to dry before being stored, usually on top of the oatmeal in wooden chests. In south-west Wales, on the other hand, they were dried in a more casual fashion, resting them against the legs of an inverted three-legged stool near the fire.

In the counties of north Wales, oatcakes were baked on a fairly regular basis well into the second half of this century. By this date it was often eaten in sandwich form by placing a large piece of oatbread between two slices of white bread. These 'sandwiches' were given colloquial names such as *brechdan gaerog, brechdan linsi, brechdan fetel* and *pioden*. It was also consumed in pottage-type dishes, crushed oatcake being the basic ingredient in the dishes known as *brwes (brose)* and *picws mali* or *siot* (shot).

In South Wales oatbread had ceased to be a staple in the diet by the early decades of the century.

Barley bread was also baked on the griddle or bakestone in certain areas in north-west Wales until the turn of this century. Prepared specifically to feed the menservants employed on the larger farms, it would be made in large quantities. Although this bread was leavened with yeast it was still considered a flat-bread and to mix a soft, pliable dough was a difficult task. Kneading was the key to its successful baking, a skill taught to every maid hired to work on these farms.

'"You have to knock hard, you know", she said "for about an hour" — to mix the flour. And then the more you knocked it the tougher it would be, and it would be a better loaf, you see. They'd rise more, the longer you did it. It was a hard job, a farm maid's work, the work of a kitchen maid in those days.'

Baking would take place on a flat-hearth in an outhouse:

'And the big griddle then, about three loaves went on this griddle. And the fire would be red hot. You'd bank it up well the night before baking, and once you'd given it a poke in the morning it would be red hot. Then bacon fat to rub on the griddle in case the bread stuck to it, and a little bit of barley meal on it afterwards'.

The dough was divided equally to form

'Large loaves. And they weren't thick, they were something like that — three or four inches then. And round, all of them the same. They were quite uncovered. And to turn them then — an oatcake slice, you know, to turn them. The oatcake slice was a useful instrument to turn bread'.

'between my two hands like that. Throw it on the griddle. Just two hands each side like that. It was like a penny between your hands. Just put it on the fire, then take the oatcake slice and give it a quarter turn. Give the loaf a quarter turn to make sure it baked all over. Then take the slice, look at it a bit, put the edge underneath it and turn it, it was ready. There was no need for it to go a heavy old yellow colour, to bake too much. I liked them to bake a nice clean white. And they were baked enough too, you know'.

In north Wales, the cakes were then transferred to a custom-made wooden or iron stand which stood in front of the fire.

'We'd lift them then and put them on the rack. Car bara we used to call it. Something like a small screen it was, in front of the fire, with small steps to it, made for the purpose. In front of the fire to finish properly, just in case they weren't done. We'd leave them there for a long time.'

They would be baked evenly for some fifteen minutes on both sides and then placed to cool, leaning against one another, edge to edge, on a stone slab, before storing.

Although the built-in wall-oven was well established in most areas during the early decades of this century, the tradition of baking on a bakestone co-existed with it. Heating this large oven would be confined to one specific day in every week and subsequently the family's supply of bread and cakes would be augmented by that which could be baked over the open fire. Flat-breads known as *cacen radell* (griddle cake) or *cacen soda* (soda cake) would be prepared and baked regularly in the counties of north Wales, and their counterparts in the southern half of the country were called *bara cri, bara crai* or *bara trw'r dŵr*. On a normal baking day it would be common practice also to bake a small leavened batch on the bakestone, while the bulk of the dough would be baked in the oven. A similar batch, fortified with sugar, lard and currants was another bakestone favourite, prepared in most areas, and was known as *cacen gri*

(speckled cake), *teisen does* (dough cake) or *teisen radell* (griddle cake). *Leicecs* (small drop scones) were baked on the bakestone as a special welcome to visitors in Merioneth and Denbighshire. A variety of pancakes were baked on Shrove Tuesday throughout the country, but more especially in Anglesey and Caernarfonshire (Gwynedd) where they prepared *crempog furum* (yeasted pancake) or *crempog wen* (pancakes made with refined flour), to be consumed by members of the family, in contrast to the *crempog surgeirch* or *bara bwff* (oatmeal based pancakes), served to the servants. Occasional labour would be employed in the larger farm-houses on that day to assist in baking a sufficient supply of each type. Pancakes were associated with birthday celebrations in most districts in south Wales, and they were given the names *ffroes, pancos* or *cramoth*. Fruit turnovers, and small, round cakes, now generally known as 'Welsh cakes', were also bakestone tea-time treats in the southern half of the country.

BARA
WAFER OATMEAL BISCUITS
SOLE MANUFACTURERS:
THE CAMBRIAN BARA & BISCUIT CO.,
LAMPETER.

Oatcake label (Welsh Folk Museum Archive)

Leavened Bread

Bread-making was one of the major weekly tasks for which the housewife would allocate a whole day. Tuesdays, Thursdays and Fridays were the regular baking days in different areas. The skill was transferred from generation to generation solely by practical experience. Despite the numerous household management books published in the eighteenth and nineteenth centuries it is unlikely that many found their way into ordinary Welsh homes. It was the lore of common sense and experience that governed the quality of bread served to most households. Baking by Welsh housewives followed a very similar pattern in most areas. Taking a large earthenware pan or a wooden kneading trough, the quantity of dough prepared for a week's baking would differ according to the size of the family. The amount of flour used would vary from 7lbs to 20lbs per baking. By the early twentieth century the majority of households would make bread from purchased white flour, although some informants recalled making mixed bread using a quantity of home-produced wheat or barley flour to fortify the refined flour. All informants noted the important factor of keeping all ingredients and utensils warm throughout the whole process — in the first instance, it was essential to warm the earthenware pan before putting the flour into it.

The type of yeast used varied slightly in different parts of the country. Many recalled using home-made liquid yeast in the rural areas whereas informants in the more urban areas bought liquid brewers' yeast from the local inn. Home-made liquid yeast was prepared in large quantities by individuals anxious to augment the family income. Known as *berman* or *burum dirwest* or *burum total*, it was sold to neighbours for approximately a penny per pint. Its strength was not equal to that of the brewers' or the compressed dried yeast and this primarily accounted for the custom of preparing the dough in the evenings and leaving it to rise overnight.

'We had an earthenware bowl. A big, earthenware bowl. Earthenware, you know. And then on a Monday night we'd bring the barm we'd call it. Yeast hadn't arrived then. Barm. We'd get it from the houses nearby. There was an old woman there who made this barm. And we'd bring it Monday night from chapel, and we'd wet the dough. And then, by Tuesday morning, it had risen up, to the top, of course.'

Some would pour the liquid yeast and a quantity of warm water into a hole in the centre of the flour, cover and leave it in a warm place to ferment overnight. Others would put the mixture in an earthenware jug and place it on a warm hob for an hour or so to 'prove' before adding it to the flour.

Alternative methods of 'proving' the less laborious compressed or dried 'German' yeast, that later became readily available in the local stores, were also noted. One preferred method was to cream the yeast with a little sugar, pour it into a well in the centre of the flour, cover with a little flour and allow it to 'prove' for a short period before proceeding to mix the dough. Another common method was to cream the yeast with a little sugar, pepper and warm water in a bowl, cover and allow it to ferment before pouring it into a well in the centre of the flour. This reactivation of the dried yeast was a sure way of discovering whether it was fit for use.

Mixing the dough followed a fairly general pattern with all informants testifying to the importance of using the correct amount of warm water of 'blood heat'. Warmer water would ferment the dough too quickly, while hot water would 'kill the yeast' *(lladd calon y berem)*. Using too much water, on the other hand, would 'drown the miller' *(boddi'r melinydd)* and give a heavy dough, while too little water would result in a hard bread.

The secret of making good quality bread, however, lay to a very large extent in the art of kneading the dough. Having gently worked in all the flour into the 'yeasty part', sides to middle, in order to bring the dough to an even consistency throughout, the kneading began. This was hard work. Usually the earthenware pan was placed in a low position, on an old chair, stool or settle, so that the process could be carried out at a comfortable level. Kneading 20lbs of flour would take some forty-five minutes. (The English noun *lady* derives from the Anglo-Saxon *hlaefdige* or *loaf-kneader*). Using both fists, the experienced would gently pound the dough, allowing air to enter and make it light and spongy. The secret, according to some, would be to knead 'until the dough sings', the light dough being full of air would squeak as it was handled. The most general observation, however, was to knead the dough until both the hands and the sides of the bowl were free of any loose flour or sticky dough.

> 'And you'd knead and knead and knead until it was a lump, and there wasn't a bit of dough left around the bowl. The bowl would become clean. Oh, the kneading was important. The more you kneaded, the better the bread would be. Then you'd put a fist in it, and cover it with a clean cloth that was quite warm. Then you'd put something over it, to keep it warm.'

Plunging a folded fist into the perfectly kneaded round lump was also common practice, again allowing more air into the dough as it finally rose in the bowl. Covering the dough in the bowl followed a general pattern, using warm blankets, shawls, newspaper or even overcoats to accelerate the process. Having used compressed yeast, large amounts of dough would take between two to three hours to rise. The bowl would be placed in a warm, draught-free position, usually on the kitchen hearth or on the settle at the side. When using liquid yeast, the process would be allowed to take place overnight.

> 'And then we had settles at home, each side of the fire, big old settles with high back to them. And there was a settle here by the side of the fire, and on the corner of this settle the bowl would be left overnight.'

By day, another more comfortable position was sought by the more inventive housewife.

> 'And you know what? Old people years ago would put the bowl — the dough — in the bed in the bedroom. And then the bedclothes would go over it like that, and it would rise in no time — after they had got out of their beds! Then it was in — I hope, it was — in a clean place, wasn't it?'

The disadvantages of allowing the dough to rise overnight were also noted. One hazard contended with during the summer months was that the dough would turn sour if left in a warm place for too long a period. Another common danger was for the dough to rise too much and consequently fall over the sides of the bowl. When this happened the dough had to be re-kneaded, thus delaying the final baking. To prevent this from

happening it was essential for the housewife to be up and about very early on bread baking day!

The final stage of dividing and moulding the dough would be carried out on a large wooden bread board *(pren bara)* or on the wooden scrub-top kitchen table. In the earlier period the dough would be moulded to form large batches for baking on the open hearth. They were baked individually in a greased and pre-heated pot-oven or beneath an inverted pan on a pre-heated griddle. With the introduction of the wall-oven, initially, loaves were baked directly on the floor of the oven, but informants recalled using old frying pans with broken handles or earthenware pots as bread-baking utensils before tins became available. Both oval and oblong tins were in general use by the post First World War period. All baking utensils were greased and pre-heated before use. The dough would be divided and moulded according to the size and number of available utensils. The top of each loaf would be marked with a sharp knife or pricked with a fork to form a symmetrical pattern. Informants were of the opinion that this custom also helped the loaf to bake evenly. To see large holes in the crumb of the bread was no credit to a 'lady'. Finally, the filled tins were placed to 'prove' on the warm hearth for a further half hour before they were placed in a pre-heated oven.

Simultaneously, some housewives would continue to keep a little dough and bake a small batch on the bakestone. This batch would be eaten fresh for tea on that day. *Bara planc, bara mân* or *bara prwmlid* were among the regional Welsh names by which it was known. Similarly, small batches would be baked on the floor of the enclosed oven. Regional variations accounted for the different names given to them — *bara bricen, torth waelod popty, torth ar fflat y ffwrn* and *torth llawr ffwrn*.

Another common baking day custom was to put aside a small quantity of dough and use it as a base for a currant bread. The usual method was to work a little lard, sugar and currants into the dough and knead it well. It was then covered and left to rise in a warm place, as for bread. Finally, it was moulded into a large loaf, placed in a tin and baked together with the ordinary bread. *Teisen fara, teisen dos cwnnad* and *teisen does* were among the more general names given to this favourite loaf.

Baking

PAN AND GRIDDLE METHOD

An extended use of the bakestone was to employ it in conjunction with an iron pan or pot to form an enclosed area for baking leavened bread. Until the beginning of the century, it was general practice in Anglesey and on the Llŷn peninsula in Caernarfonshire (Gwynedd) to bake leavened barley bread beneath an inverted iron pan on the bakestone or griddle. With a tripod stand supporting the bakestone on the flat-hearth over a low fire, glowing embers would also be piled over the inverted pan, thus enclosing the loaf in a warm chamber. Several bakestones with inverted pans would be used simultaneously on the larger farms. In Anglesey it is known for this particular method of baking to be practised in a sheltered position in the open air, with the bakestone and inverted pan buried in a bed of red-hot ashes. A slow combustible fuel, usually peat, would be used for this purpose, but furze, gorse, straw and chaff were also suitable alternatives. This baking method was described as *pobi allan* (literally, baking outside) or *pobi yn y baw* (literally, baking in dirt), and the bread itself was known as *bara gradell* (griddle bread) or *bara cetlan* (kettle bread) in Anglesey, and as *bara dan badell* (bread beneath a pan) or *bara padell a gradell* (griddle and pan bread) in Caernarfonshire.

> *'Pan and griddle, what a baking that was! You had a griddle, a round griddle like the surface of a small table. Then you had something with three legs, a tripod to hold this griddle. And then you'd wipe that clean, and rub it with grease, and then sprinkle a little flour over the whole surface. Then you had a pan, a cast iron pan — you'd have heated that to start with, you know. And then you'd put the loaf on the griddle and the pan on top of it, and then a good fire. You'd light a fire underneath it, and a fire on top. They used to have turf years ago. That would last a long time. I used gorse, fine gorse, and fragments of gorse — you know the fine stuff that comes from the gorse. Then these gorse fragments were put round it and on top, and smaller fragments underneath. And that was it, you'd leave it then. Yes, and you'd go there afterwards and look, "Oh, is it ready yet?". And so that's how we used to use the pan and griddle. Oh, it was a lovely loaf. Much better than an oven loaf.'*

With the establishment of the built-in cast iron wall oven in these two counties during the early decades of this century, this tradition of baking barley bread was transferred into the oven. The covered loaf was now placed on the floor of the pre-heated oven. Wheaten bread or mixed-flour bread gradually superseded the barley bread and the loaves were then baked in upstanding tins in the normal way. Hence the baking-under method in this area became extinct.

The corresponding method employed in north Pembrokeshire and south Cardiganshire (Dyfed) was that of using an inverted iron pot or cauldron over the bakestone and the bread was described as *bara dan cidl* (literally, bread beneath the kettle). These two methods of baking located in the extreme western regions in north and south Wales can be traced to Cornwall, where two traditional variants on the 'baking under' method survived into the later years of the nineteenth century. Some households used a 'kettle' — a three-legged iron crock or bowl, others favoured a 'baker' the name given to a plain, round pot which was similar to an outsize frying-pan. Whichever type of covering pot was used, the prepared dough was laid on a stout round iron griddle, ready heated on a trivet thrust into the centre of the open hearth with the burning peat or turf underneath. Having discussed the covering pots in Wales, it is evident that the equivalent to the 'baker' was employed in north Wales and that of the 'kettle' was confined to the southern region.

POT-OVEN METHOD

Coinciding with these two traditional variants, however, another baking-pot or pot-oven tradition was evident in the hinterland of Wales. An observer in west Montgomeryshire, writing in 1887, describing the typical house in the district, states *'weithiau gwneid ffwrn hefyd, ond y rhan amlaf cresid y bara mewn crochan pobi'* (literally, sometimes an oven was built, but generally the bread was baked in the baking pot). A deep, flat-bottomed pot with straight tapering sides and a closely fitting lid was used extensively for baking bread in Cardiganshire, Carmarthenshire (Dyfed), Merioneth (Gwynedd), Denbighshire (Clwyd), and Breconshire and Montgomeryshire (Powys). Informants from this extensive region of Wales testified that the pot-oven was the only type of oven available to many households until the later decades of the nineteenth century, and that the pot-oven in Carmarthenshire, Cardiganshire and Breconshire was *ffwrn fach* (literally, small oven), while it was known simply as *crochan pobi* (literally, baking pot) in Montgomeryshire and parts of Denbighshire, but the name *cetel* (literally, kettle) was adopted in parts of Denbighshire and in the whole of Merioneth.

The most general method of employing it, usually on a flat hearth or in a sheltered position outside the house, was to rest it directly on glowing embers, or on a tripod over the open fire. Alternatively, the pot was suspended over the fire from a pot-hook and chain. With the

Baking bread in a pot-oven: Mrs. E. Rogers, Ffair Rhos, Dyfed

introduction of the built-up iron grate, it is known for the pot to be positioned beneath the grate itself, where the glowing embers were raked from the grate on to the lid of the pot. Informants in Breconshire and Denbighshire had witnessed this practice. Baking in the pot-oven was an acquired art, as described by an octogenarian who recalled her own mother's skill:

> *'Pot loaf. The old lady, my mother, she was exceptional with the pot loaf.'*

The pot and lid were pre-heated before placing the risen dough inside it.

> *'You'd put it to warm, you know, and grease the bottom of it. You'd let it heat up before putting the dough loose in the oven then. You'd make it a small round one, a small round piece, you know. Gosh, it was nice!'*

Peat would be the preferred fuel for use with the pot-oven method, although straw, gorse and wood were again used according to availability. Live embers were placed on the lid of the pot as well as beneath it so that the loaf would be completely enclosed with heat. The building of the embers on the lid had to follow a certain procedure to ensure even baking, allowing an hour or more for a small batch.

> *'A peat fire. I never tried it on a coal fire. The coal fire would go out before it baked, you know. Oh, a small fire. You'd let it burn — to settle, we'd say, you know — let the fire settle before we'd do it. You'd have a red fire to put on the top of the lid and everything then. You had to put a small ring around it, you know. There's a little bit of grooving on the lid of the (pot) oven. Well inside that, you put it round like that. You never put much on the top. Well if you put it in the middle now, the loaf would burn in the middle, you know. The middle rises more doesn't it? You put it on the sides, and it baked the sides and all then. Oh, it wouldn't be long, you see. We could only make a small loaf, you see. You didn't make a big loaf, filling the oven. Oh, about an hour and a half, perhaps. That would be quite enough.'*

Another suitable fuel, used in conjunction with pot-oven baking in certain areas of Wales, was dried cow dung. Available for its collecting, especially during the summer months it provided families with a clean slow combustible heat.

'My mother's grandmother, in the summer she would go around the fields where the cattle had been grazing, with a stick in her hand and a home-made wicker basket on her arm. And what she'd do if the sun was hot was to take her stick and turn the dung — perhaps it would be a bit damp underneath — and turn it over so that it would dry out. And she'd go back the following day and collect it all, filling the basket. And that's what she had underneath to bake the pot loaf. She'd put this dung under the pot — there was a gap and legs under it — and then she'd make the loaf, put it in, close the lid on this pot then, and put some of the dung on top of the lid. It came over the edges a little. And she'd light that, and then it would heat up. The loaf would bake up and down and on the sides. Baked in the pot, because it wasn't in a tin or anything, you know, and the pot was clean enough. A nice round little loaf. It must have been good, you know.'

The pot-oven was gradually superseded by the built-in brick wall-ovens in most houses in the early decades of the century. Informants, however, recalled their reluctance to relinquish the pot-oven during the period of transition. They referred to the superior attributes of the one loaf which they continued to bake in the pot while the bulk of the bread was baked in the wall-oven.

A distinctive feature of this transitional period was recorded in north Pembrokeshire (Dyfed). An iron pot was placed laterally in a suitable aperture in the kitchen wall, and was fitted with two iron shelves and a custom-made iron door. A fire-box was built beneath it and a flue-vent provided above, thus introducing the *ffwrn gidl* (an improvised pot-oven) as a fore-runner to the cast iron wall-ovens that were later found in the districts of Newport and Brynberian.

Mrs Patty John, Mynachlog-ddu, Dyfed, baking in a pot oven

Bread Ovens — Types and Location

The combination of the bakestone and inverted iron pot for baking bread may have been a prototype of the early bread ovens. Early clay and brick-built ovens were dome-shaped and are known to have been introduced to Britain at a very early date. The Celts, who arrived in Britain during the early Iron Age, used clay domes to parch corn and probably to bake bread. Roman settlers brought further innovations to Britain, including their bread oven. The usual type was a fixed oven with a domed roof of rubble and tiles and a flue in front. Wood or charcoal was burnt inside for a time and then raked out so that bread and cakes could be baked in the heated chamber. In the medieval period, such ovens were to be found in the manor or monastery. The peasant was allowed to take dough to be baked in the manorial ovens on condition that he gave a portion of it in payment.

It is known that wall-ovens, either built-in examples of stone or fire-brick, or more portable ones of clay were in south-east Wales as early as the beginning of the seventeenth century. The use of the wall-oven spread very gradually to most parts of Wales, but it was not until the late nineteenth century that the baking oven became a common feature in most large farmhouses. However, it seems that the built-in brick wall-oven did not infiltrate as far as some areas in north-east Wales. Farmhouses continued to use the pan and griddle or pot oven until they had solid fuel ranges with a cast iron oven.

A portable clay-oven was found in Glamorgan farmhouses in the early seventeenth century. It was a domed structure made of coarse clay banded together with gravel and frequently decorated with applied bands and fingernail impressions. Examples bear a Bideford maker's mark. Bideford in north Devon was the centre of a large-scale pottery industry, in its day rivalling Staffordshire as one of the major British centres of earthenware production. The industry was centred on the three main towns of Bideford, which had a source of gravel still used today by the cement industry, Fremington, which lay on the band of reddish clay of excellent potting quality, and the port of Barnstaple. North Devon clay ovens were certainly being imported into Wales in the seventeenth century, and were most probably imported a century earlier; the trade continued for a long time, almost up to the time the ovens ceased to be made in the early twentieth century. In 1883 Llewelyn Jewitt wrote in his *Ceramic Art of Great Britain* that the ovens made in the Crocker pottery in Bideford,

> *"are, and for generations have been in much repute in Devon and Cornwall, and in the Welsh districts, and the bread baked in them is said to have a sweeter and more wholesome flavour than when baked in ordinary ovens".*

The last ovens to be produced at the Truro pottery were made in 1937 and were identical to ones made over three centuries before.

The built-in stone or brick oven, however, was far more common than the clay oven in Wales. The earlier examples were found either inside the large fireplace or to one side of it, but examples are very difficult to date. A seventeenth-century date seems probable for the earliest stone or brick ovens in Glamorgan also, except perhaps for the large houses like Beaupre — there is no contemporaneous oven at St. Fagans Castle, for instance, in existence by 1590. The early ovens seem to have had thin slabs of stone as a door, plastered around with mud to keep them in place when the oven was in use. They are usually without a flue — in other words, the fire was lit inside, or hot ashes were used.

However, the built-in baking oven did not supersede the pot-oven tradition in the hinterland of Wales until the late nineteenth and early twentieth centuries. As already indicated, the earlier built-in ovens found in Glamorgan and Gwent were usually located either inside the large fireplaces or to one side of them. This was not always the case in the later, nineteenth century examples. In Cardiganshire it was recorded that bread was baked in a wall oven which might be mounted in the wall of the back kitchen or of an outhouse. This outhouse or outside kitchen became a common feature of Welsh life. The separate building frequently housed a baking oven and a copper for boiling water and it was used for baking bread, washing, brewing and preparing food for animal consumption. In many areas in north Wales, this building was known as *briws* (literally, brew-house) or *tŷ popty* (literally, oven house) while in most parts of south-west Wales it was known as *tŷ ffwrn* (literally, oven house) or *tŷ pair* (literally, boiler house). This terminology variation is evident when it is realised that the general Welsh term for a bread oven in north Wales is *popty* (literally, bakehouse) and its counterpart in south Wales is *ffwrn* (oven) or *ffwrn wal* (wall-oven).

Most of these 'outside' kitchens with built-in ovens seem to be nineteenth century in date and contain an oven with a cast-iron door. Such structures are, however, recorded in south-east Wales from an earlier period: White House, Clytha, Gwent, had an oven in an outside building dating to the late seventeenth century, and there is such a structure, at least seventeenth century, if not earlier in date, at Flemingston in Glamorgan. Indeed, outside bakehouses were common in Glamorgan in the eighteenth century, though, for some reason not yet clear, more bakehouses are known from Gower than from elsewhere in the country. The spread of the outside bakehouse may be connected with the spread of the baking-oven itself.

Baking in a farmhouse wall-oven: Miss M. Jones, Llanuwchllyn, Gwynedd

THE USE OF THE BRICK WALL-OVEN

As soon as the dough had been set aside to rise, the next major task was to fire and heat the oven. To quote William Cobbett in the chapter on making bread in his publication *Cottage Economy* (1822)

> *'In the mean while the oven is to be heated and this is much more than half the art of the operation'.*

To heat the oven to the correct temperature was of paramount importance, a skill which was again attained by observation and experience.

The brick ovens were constructed so that each brick was precisely placed to form an arched or a beehive-shaped cavity, the floor of which was also of brick. There were no sharp corners or side flues and the mouth of the oven was closed by suitable cover or door. The cavity would be filled with dry fuel and, when fired, the flames would encircle the whole surface area.

the oven, spread it out. And then it would turn into red embers, and you'd leave the embers there all across the oven . . . Well, we had something like an old fashioned rake now to spread it about, to scatter the peat. Spread it like ashes over it like this, you know. And then leave it for a bit. And the bricks would have all changed colour and gone white'.

The methods employed to determine the exact temperature of the oven varied slightly from one household to another. This one informant observed the colour of the bricks inside the oven. White hot bricks were, in her experience, the key to successful baking. The more general method of determining it, however, was for the housewife to lean slightly towards the oven, push her right arm into the heated chamber and hold it there for a certain number of seconds while she counted slowly from one to ten, or doubling the pace and counting up to twenty. A cooler oven would give heavy, doughy loaves while a hotter oven would provide the family with the inevitable burnt offerings.

'Oh, we'd call it the old baking oven, you see. Baking oven. It was an oven made from bricks. It was brick on the inside, and it would redden. You'd fill it, and there was a big roar. A wood fire. You'd keep it full. Then when that had died down, you'd put your hand in to see if there was enough heat there. If you could keep your hand there for about ten seconds, that was enough. You knew it was right then, you see. And then you'd rake the embers out. You had a little thing that we called a scraper. You'd clean the bottom of the oven out then, clean it all until the floor was clean. But the oven was boiling, of course. Hot. And in with the bread then quickly. And shut it, and seal it.'

Another informant recalls how her mother taught her 'to know her oven' and observe the colour of the wood embers, the colour of the bricks as they rose in temperature as well as the all-important count-up to twenty as the final test:

'You'd light the wood now, and that wood had to burn until the embers were white. And you knew the oven. It would become ready for baking, as the embers died. It would go all white. Inside the oven. White! And Mam now would count to twenty, with her hand on the surface of the oven like this. Twenty. I can see her — hundreds of times counting there. "That's it, girls. Come on! Ready!". We'd put the bread in.'

Housewives throughout Wales continued to follow the same procedure well into the first half of the twentieth century. Primarily, they sought sufficient fuel to fill the oven a week in advance so that it could be dried in the warm chamber at the end of a current baking session. Thus, they were confident that it was ready for firing the following week. They could not afford to contend with a damp supply of fuel on baking day.

The fuel most commonly used in Wales was wood — elm, beech or oak being the most suitable, although gorse or broom were known to be used in some hilly regions. However, peat, harvested for use as fuel on many moorland farms, proved more suitable for baking, as stated by a housewife from Llanuwchllyn, near Bala, in Merioneth (Gwynedd):

'We had a big oven years ago, heated by peat. Much better, a peat fire. Oh yes, it was. It heated properly right through. With wood, well, you'd only have little bits of the oven heating here and there. Oh, it would take an hour to heat. And then, after it had heated, you had to scatter it all over

Freshly baked bread at Farrier's Cottage, Rhyd-y-car, Merthyr Tudful, Mid Glamorgan: Mrs. Susannah Rowlings

To remove the dying embers and thoroughly clean the oven floor was essential when all loaves were baked directly on the heated bricks. When tins became available this task did not have to be executed as thoroughly, but if the oven had become too hot, mopping the floor with a long-handled, wet 'dolly' or 'ladi' helped to reduce the temperature. (This tool would be a mop made of rags or sacking.)

'Setting the oven' — the term used for placing the loaves in position inside the oven, was a task that had to be done quickly and smoothly, so that the oven could be sealed as soon as possible thus retaining the heat inside it. Great care had to be taken when handling the risen dough. Each individual tin would be placed on the peel (a long handled spade-like tool) and placed in position inside the oven. Tins of different shapes and sizes were set as pieces in a jig-saw puzzle. 'You had to know your oven'. Finally, small batches or pot loaves were placed near the mouth of the oven which were later given as baking-day treats to the children.

Ovens fitted with a fixed cast-iron door were readily closed. In this context housewives frequently referred to the custom of reserving some of the warm embers for use as a 'draught excluder' on the oven ledge, placed tightly against the closed door. This barrier helped to conserve the heat and prevented any cold air from entering the oven.

'Seven loaves of bread. And we'd shut the door on them and leave them there for two hours. An iron door. We'd shut it tight so that no air would get at them. So there was no need to touch the door or anything once the bread was put in.'

Earlier brick-ovens, however, were closed with a stone or slate slab which had been cut to size so that it fitted tightly over the mouth of the oven. Informants from many districts, both in the south-east and south-west counties had vivid recollections of placing these doors in position. To seal or 'pad' around a stone door was another all-important skill acquired by experience. In some households, old rags or paper would be used:

'Plenty of paper everywhere, wetted and squeezed up. It was like putty. And you'd put a real good dab of that all round. Pad the oven. And no air would get in then, you see. It was airtight then. And you know, when you took that down, it was dry. As dry as a bone. But I remember well, I remember having to wet the paper like that. And then, rags after that. Rags would be used very often. You had rags. And they would last longer than the paper, of course. So that was padding. And that was the last task, after the bread had gone in. That was the last task.'

When available, clay would be used. It would be easier to handle and was probably found to be a more effective sealer. It also acted as a 'tell-tale', signifying to the housewife the opportune moment to open the oven and find perfectly baked bread. To open the oven too soon could prove disastrous, consequently giving the housewife a week's supply of flat, doughy bread.

'And we'd put the stone, and old stone slab over the oven. And dubbing right around here. Clay, she had to have the clay ready! And the wetter it was, it would dry like a cinder,
you see. And you'd see — Mam would say "It's almost time to take the bread out!" "How do you know, Mam?" "Well, you see, that clay is almost completely dry", she said. And she was right! When the clay dried, it was like a cork. It was time for you to open the oven. She was right too. Oh, you can't beat experience. We'd open the oven carefully, and oh, you'd see the bread! Beautiful!'

The approved baking period varied slightly according to the size of individual ovens, but usually it took approximately one and a half hours to bake a whole batch of bread. The baked loaves were then taken out of the oven again with the aid of the oven peel. At this stage, it was general custom by most housewives to test each individual loaf as it was carefully removed from the tin. A gentle tap or knock with the knuckles on the sides and bottom crust resulting in a hollow, resonant sound signified a well baked loaf and a sure reward for their hard day's work. Finally, the loaves were placed on their sides or in an inverted position on a wooden surface and allowed to cool. Freshly-baked bread would soon become mouldy if stored while it was warm. Covered with a clean linen cloth, the loaves were usually left to cool overnight and then stored in a suitable receptacle. An earthenware crock or dough bowl with a custom-made wooden lid was chiefly used although wooden bread racks suspended from the kitchen ceiling were provided in the larger farmhouses.

The use of the brick oven was not confined to bread-baking only. It played a far wider role in a household's economy as indeed it provided more than 24 hours heat. While the bread was in the oven the housewife would promptly prepare some fruit tarts, currant-breads and puddings. The bricks retained heat for a long period, but possibly a second, minor firing would be reqired to boost the temperature before setting the oven for the second time. Furthermore, at the end of the day, a large bowlful of rice-pudding was generally placed in the oven and allowed to bake slowly overnight, a treat enjoyed by all ages. On the following day, the remaining heat was further utilised — the oven now being used as a warm cupboard in which the family's weekly laundry was aired. Finally, it would be re-filled with fuel for drying in preparation for the following week's baking marathon.

Communal and Commercial Bakehouses

The tradition of home baking persisted in most Welsh homes well into the twentieth century with members of families strongly objecting to 'boughten bread', commonly known in Welsh as *bara starfo* (bread for starving) or *bara ffenast* (window bread). The built-in type wall-oven was kept in use in rural areas well into the mid-decades of the century. With the growth of both villages and industrial and market towns, however, cooking facilities in the home changed radically. The small ovens incorporated in the iron kitchen ranges which were installed in most urban homes in the late nineteenth and early twentieth centuries proved both unsatisfactory and inadequate for baking bread for large families. They were not regarded as 'good bakers of bread'. Reporting on the iron oven in 1855, Eliza Acton wrote in *Modern Cookery*:

'. . . though exceedingly convenient from the facility which they afford for baking at all hours on the day, do not in general answer well for bread, unless it be made into very small loaves or rolls, as the surface becomes hardened and browned long before the heat has sufficiently penetrated to the centre of the dough'.

Another domestic economist, writing in a publication entitled *Lady Bountiful's Legacy* (ed. John Timbs, 1868) was of a similar opinion:

'The iron ovens attached to kitchen ranges, in most cases, will spoil the bread attempted to be baked in them as it will be either unevenly baked or altogether burnt'.

He stipulated

'. . . if, therefore, a family possess not a brick oven, the bread should be sent to the baker's'.

Esther Copley in *The Complete Cottage Cookery* (1849), advised still further on the economy of using the service offered by the local baker:

'Persons who live near to an honest baker may find it as economical to send their bread to his oven; the usual charge is ½d. a loaf'.

By and large, bakers were not established as commercial traders in Welsh villages and towns until the early decades of this century. The housewife continued to play a key role in providing bread for the family and was assisted to overcome the inadequacy of the small iron ovens. In the first instance, builders in urban areas provided communal brick ovens built on convenient sites to serve a specific number of houses only. Ironmasters such as Richard Crawshay, who built 29 houses for the iron-miners of the Rhyd-y-car iron ore mine near Merthyr Tudful in Mid Glamorgan in the early nineteenth century, eventually provided three communal ovens to serve this particular community. This arrangement was typical of many streets and areas throughout the industrial towns and villages of both north and south Wales.

In general these communal ovens were built within a simple, detached, single storey building, usually located at the end of a terrace of houses. They would be managed in an identical fashion to the domestic models already discussed. Every family would be allocated a specific day when they were granted sole use of the oven situated in close proximity to their home.

'They were bringing their own heating sticks, and they did make a little pile in the middle and they'd put coal around. Inside the oven. And then my mother was keeping the corlac (rake) in 'er back, see, and then before she'd put the bread in, she'd spread it all around with the corlac (and) scrape it all out then . . . And she put 'er 'and in then to see, 'cos my mother was always baking lovely, and a few used to ask 'er, "Come and put your 'and in now, Mary Ann, to see if it's warm enough." She knew by the feeling of it, yes. So indeed, the bread was going in then now. I couldn't tell you how long, but she knew the time it was due to come out. Oh, but what beautiful bread it was! Six large loaves. And we used to wait then for us to 'ave the warm crust off of them. Lovely bread, beautiful bread. And my mother then 'ad a big spade (peel) then to pull 'em out one by one, see, and then we used

Baking day at the village bakery, Llanelidan, near Rhuthun, Clwyd

to put them on the wall then. The walls were whitewashed. Outside. Everybody, not only my mother. They all used to put them on the wall outside for 'em to cool a bit before they'd (put them) in a lovely big clean pan in the pantry on the stone, with a big white cloth over it.'

An alternative arrangement would be to appoint one man to manage the communal oven which served a specific number of families within the community. He would be paid a set fee, usually one penny per loaf of bread or cake, per baking session.

These communal, end-of-terrace ovens proved to be the precursors of the larger custom-built bakehouses whereby 'professional' bakers set up business in urban villages and towns to provide the local community strictly with a baking facility. On attaining suitable premises, Welsh entrepreneurs built large brick ovens as commercial enterprises. Customers were invited to bring their home-prepared dough to them and pay the resident baker for his service. Derwen Bakehouse, built in Aberystwyth, Dyfed in 1900 represents this type of

Mrs. Catherine Jane Evans (nee Jenkins) who managed Derwen Bakery until the business closed in 1924

Mrs. Chris Aston (baker) kneading dough at Derwen Bakery, Welsh Folk Museum, St. Fagans

business. They were established in most areas throughout the country and were well-frequented by local residents.

Large numbers of elderly Welsh housewives have vivid memories of their mothers or grandmothers taking advantage of their local baker's oven. Many of them were of the same opinion that to heat up the small iron oven in the home proved expensive; furthermore, it was not 'a good baker of bread'. Using coal to stoke up the oven to attain the required high temperature for the sake of baking a day or two's supply of bread was not profitable. As one stipulated:

'. . . but it became cheaper to take them to the bakehouse, you know. "Communal" you'd call them today. She'd make four at a time'.

Another recalled how her mother would depend on the local bakehouse under certain circumstances only:

'Sometimes, when she wasn't well, or perhaps we couldn't have coal or something — not much money — then we'd take

the dough, my brother and I, in the clothes basket, a handle each, to the bakehouse'.

A baker's daughter who had assisted her parents in their family bakehouse during the First World War period confirmed that housewives from a large catchment area in the Swansea valley (West Glamorgan) would take regular advantage of the baking facility offered to them:

'Why did these people bring bread to you? Didn't they have ovens?' 'Well, no, I think — it was too much trouble, I think, to heat the oven, you know. And there weren't many gas stoves and electric stoves then, were there? Say around 1916, 1917 like that, there weren't many ovens about. They'd bring about half a dozen loaves, perhaps, and then they would last for the week. And we didn't charge much. We only charged a penny a loaf you see. Yes, and a penny for a tart.'

Many of the successful 'bakehouses' gradually developed into larger commercial concerns, whereby the baker built up his trade by preparing his own dough and baking bread to sell to customers over a fairly wide area. Commercial bakeries were established here and there in the larger Welsh villages and towns during the

Baking bread at Derwen Bakery, Welsh Folk Museum

Heating the oven at Derwen Bakery, Welsh Folk Museum

early decades of the century. Even at this date, however, many of these bakers still continued to provide the housewife with a baking facility. Side by side with baking his own bread supply, the baker would allocate specific hours or days when he would accept dough from customers for 'public baking'.

Having baked his own bread in the morning, one baker referred to the pattern of allocating the afternoon for 'the outsiders':

'Well, the batches were out about eleven every morning, about eleven, half past eleven. And the bread out about twelve perhaps, you see. It was all over by about dinner time, see. And we'd bake for the outsiders in the afternoon, you understand. Say — "bring your bread by two o'clock, make your bread by six, as it suits you, you see?" And then we'd bake tarts for some people'.

Other bakers limited their services to certain hours on specific week days:

'William Huws' bakehouse, as we used to call it. And we'd bake every — wait a minute — Monday and Wednesday with William Huws. Friday night, there was a small old bakehouse — you'd get to it through Stryd Bach — Robert Jones' bakehouse we used to call it. Friday night, we'd take the dough there'.

The work area within the bakehouses was sparsely furnished with the basic requirements for managing the dough and the tins. Cleanliness was of paramount importance and great care was taken to scrub clean all work surfaces daily:

'The bakehouse was a sizeable room, with tables right around, of course, the shelves. Wooden tables and wooden shelves, and we had to scrub those every day, you see. They were like the driven snow, girl. Yes. We would whitewash the bakehouse every three months, you know. Whitewash it. The walls. And we had red tiles on the floor. We'd wash out every day, and the tables were scrubbed every day. And that was the last job we'd do, scrubbing the tables and washing the floor out'.

Firing these large ovens followed a similar pattern to that already described for the domestic models, and generally the fuel used was wood. The experienced baker was also adept at managing and 'knowing' his own oven. To heat the oven to the required temperature was, of course, a skill gained by experience only. One baker from Anglesey in Gwynedd explained how he knew the oven was hot enough to use:

The Arran Oatcakes' Shop, Bala, Gwynedd, c. 1920 (by courtesy of Gwynedd Archives Service)

'There wasn't any kind of thermometer or anything, but you'd do it with your hand. You learnt to do it with your hand. You'd open the oven door and put your hand in, bare. You knew. When the oven was ready you'd feel the heat going like a glove over your hand. It would grasp you. But if the oven wasn't hot, you could hold your hand there for — it wouldn't heat at all. But if the oven was hot, you could feel it moving up your arm, as if someone was putting on a glove. And you'd know that the oven was ready.'
'And what if it was too hot?'

'Well, you'd know that as well. The hairs on your arm would get singed a little. You would know. Then you'd wash it, a bit wetter, to dampen it down a little bit. But, you see, you'd wash it, and as soon as you had washed the oven, you'd put the bread in'.

The later, more sophisticated bakehouse ovens, however, were fired with coal or coke and thus were fitted with a built-in fire chamber beneath or at the side of the oven. Heat would be drawn towards and around the oven and regulated with flues and the temperature recorded on a thermometer usually fitted externally on the oven door.

Carrying the dough from the home to the bakehouse was a delicate task. Having risen in the warmth of the hearth, it would have to be covered with a flannel or thick cloth and carried quickly as the cold air would check its rising. When the dough was given out to be baked the general custom in the counties of north Wales was to take it in one lump and the baker instructed to divide it into specific shaped loaves:

'When William Huw took your dough — it would be in a clean flour sack, with a white cloth around it in case you got flour all over you. Then William Huws would say "Well, how many do you want today? Two or three loaves?" A batch and two tin loaves or two loaves — as we wanted — as Mam had said.
It was like a big kitchen. You — where the oven was — and I'm talking now about where he used to handle the dough and cut the bread into the tins — one side like this was clean tins. And you know, it was necessary to grease each tin, in case the dough stuck to it, wasn't it? Well now, one side was like that, it had these tins. Each one ready for its loaf. Then, along here there was a big, long table where he took the dough and cut it. It was a white table like the snow, too, and he had plenty of flour on it, when he was cutting the dough'.

The preferred pattern in the counties of south Wales, on the other hand, was for customers to mould the dough at home and place it in tins before taking it to the bakehouse. These loaves were readily identified by both the baker and the customers alike:

'We'd put every loaf on top of its own tin, you know. In case there'd be a mistake. Say now, some people would bring their own bread in to be baked, you understand. Some would mark their tins, of course, you know. They'd put D.J. or A.R. or something like that. Then you knew who was who bringing the bread by the tins, you see. And you'd put the loaf that had been baked on top of that tin, you see. You'd take it out of the tin and put it on top of the tin, otherwise it would sweat when it was left inside you see, and it would go soft. And we'd take every loaf out of its tin and put them on top of these tins there on the table. And they'd come to fetch their bread afterwards, of course'.

The baker who took in customers' dough for moulding and baking in his own tins also devised a fool-proof method of identifying all the individual customers bread:

'And, you know, it was comical — everybody knew and recognised his own dough! Why? you say. When William Huws took your dough he would — he had a tin, like a loaf tin, and that full of tallies. Then he would give you a tally, and put — if you had three loaves, he'd put a tally on each loaf. Then he had a tally just the same to give to me as well. Then when we went to get the bread, "the tallies with this number, look!". There were like six tallies, you see. In each pile, each one had six. Then there'd be a number, you see. Say there was 1, 2, 3 on the three that went into our bread — well, we'd have three tallies to go home with, 1, 2, 3. He knew then that those were our loaves, you see'.

However, some customers would have their own method of identification despite the baker's tally system.

'And Gran would take a piece of paper like this, and write her name — Margiad Wiliam — put it in the side of the loaf. And there were tallies to be had. They'd give you tallies. But Gran didn't have much faith in tallies. She wanted to put her name, Margiad Wiliam, on the bread. She'd make four at a time'.

Setting a large oven was a major task which had to be accomplished at great speed. Individual bakers had their set methods according to the types of loaves baked together in the one baking session. One baker described his method of using a long-handled peel to put the loaves in position:

'You'd start in one corner. You had to have a system, you see. And then you came along the side. Then you worked across and forwards until you'd come — it takes about a quarter of an hour to twenty minutes to fill it. It did. And that as fast as you could do it. Tins first, and then by the door there'd be the small loaves and cobs and brown bread and pan loaves.'
'And what about the batch loaves?'
'Well, they were in the centre of the oven, in the middle of the tins. You had to have a plan for filling it, you see. You filled it like that until it was square. Then it looked really beautiful!'

Baking fees were minimal but they provided the baker with a well-earned income. A penny a loaf was quoted

Owen (D. W. Teviotdale) Bakers with their horse-drawn bread-carts, North Parade, Aberystwyth, Dyfed, c. 1915 (by courtesy of Stewart Williams Publishers, Barry)

as being the normal charge at the turn of the century. Baking Christmas cakes, however, proved a little more expensive:

'We only charged a penny a loaf, you see. Yes, and a penny for a tart. And for a pudding too. But Christmas cake — Christmas started three weeks before Christmas in our house, because the cake was being baked, you know. And people bringing their cakes there. It would be a loaf cake. They'd bring about half a dozen loaves at a time, you know. Some would bake their cake very early. And others, later, of course. Some would bake their cake about three weeks before Christmas, while others would do it nearer Christmas, you see.'
'And baking that would cost more?'
'Yes, tuppence. Tuppence.'
'And they would take longer to bake, of course.'
'Oh yes, I'll tell you, we'd put the first lot in at six o'clock in the morning. Cakes at Christmas time now. Then we'd bake again at ten, and again at four perhaps. We'd finish then. And we'd do that, say — Father would watch that the oven wasn't too hot, you see. Say now, Tuesday, he wouldn't bake

J. H. Redwood, Abergavenny, delivery van, c. 1914 (by courtesy of Stewart Williams Publishers, Barry)

a Christmas cake at all, because it was too hot. Well, it had cooled down a bit by Thursday and Wednesday, you see. He'd bake some on a Wednesday and a few on a Thursday. So that the cake wouldn't burn, because a rich cake like that burns more easily than bread, you see, doesn't it? Yeast cake most people made for Christmas, you see'.

Children played a prominent role in transporting the dough to the bakehouse and collecting the bread at a given time:

'Oh yes, we'd always take the bread to William Huws after dinner, on the way to school. And then we'd leave the flour sack and the white cloth there ready. We'd go home to have tea first, then we'd take the basket — we had a clean clothes basket — to fetch the bread. And then . . . the sack that had held the dough and the white cloth would always have been rolled up by William Huws. And put in the middle like that. Then the loaves, after he had taken them — they had always cooled a bit by the time we had them — were put like that, and like that, in the basket. And then there were two little

31

The Derwen Bakery Shop at the Welsh Folk Museum with Mrs. Chris Aston, resident baker, 1990

white cloths. We'd be one at each end holding the basket, and this little white cloth would go over the bread. And the thing that had carried the dough to the bakehouse was in the middle, of course. Yes'.

Another informant recalls calling at the bakehouse after school in the afternoon and given a special treat by the baker. She and her brother having taken the dough to the bakehouse in a clothes basket on their way to school, they would return to collect the loaves on their way home:

'It would be a penny a loaf for baking them. And we'd carry them home in the basket. And in case we started to make

holes in the loaf, trying to eat on the way home from school,
Dic would make a small loaf for us. Yes, he would. For my
brother and myself. From the dough. On the sly that was'.

Bakehouses at the turn of the century were not only regarded strictly as workshops or business places; they also served as community centres. Like the cobbler's shop or the village smithy, the bakehouse was a popular place for social gatherings. Young girls and boys would meet there as they went to collect their bread. A baker's daughter recalls this happy time:

'Oh dear, dear, that was a lovely time. And you know, it was
a happy time, when the people used to come in to get their
bread. Oh, Mam would shout at me, "Come on, you've been
long enough chatting out there now!" The girls coming in,
you know, and the boys coming in to fetch — They'd make it
an excuse, you see, to come into the bakehouse to have a chat.
Yes, to have a little chat and a little gossip, you know. Oh, a
happy time.'
'Did they have somewhere to sit down?'
'Yes, we had a bench, you see. We had a bench to sit down.
Yes. That's it — all the gossip then, you see. And Mam
losing her temper then, of course!'
'Was the place open till late at night then?'
'Well, say until around eight o'clock, nine o'clock'.

Children were known to have long ears at that time, as always, and were not given a very warm reception at such gatherings:

'There was a social side to the bakehouse, I'm sure, was
there?'
'Oh yes, certainly. And do you know, a crowd would collect,
having left their dough there — we children going to school
weren't able to stay, but when we went to collect the bread
there was some fun. And we used to like to stay and listen.
And I remember a very amusing character used to come to
Robert Jones' bakehouse. He's been dead for years, poor
thing. He was a painter. Oh, he'd tell some tales! And we
wouldn't want to go from there with the bread. And
sometimes they were things we shouldn't have heard, as
children! Old Miss Jones and Robert Jones would throw us
out on those occasions'.

The old brick oven has played a prominent role in the lengthy story of bread-making. From Roman times to the early decades of the twentieth century, the texture of its bread was second to none. The oven's special attributes are described by an Anglesey baker:

'You were telling me earlier that there was quite a difference
between an oven like this and the modern electric ones. What
is the difference?'
'Oh, well, the old brick oven, it draws some water — the
bricks draw the water. But these modern ovens, the water
goes back into the loaf. Because of the metal. It throws it
back. And so the crust doesn't break like the crust of an old
brick oven loaf. The crust of an electric oven loaf, it wants to
stretch. That's the difference. Like glass and cotton wool,
say'.

Many commercial bakers in Welsh towns and villages continued to use their old brick ovens well into the first half of this century. Some were converted so that they could be fired with coal, coke or gas. Others were replaced with more sophisticated models with side or back furnaces, which were also fitted with external thermometers. Small family businesses grew as transport facilities improved, more especially in rural areas, in the immediate post Second World War period. Bakers' vans travelled some ten to fifteen miles radius to deliver freshly baked bread to both village shops and isolated farmhouses and cottages. On average, the 'baker' became a regular visitor to most rural areas twice or three times a week. This service led to the gradual decline of the art of home baking. Having experienced a flour shortage during the war years, housewives readily purchased bread which was delivered to their doorstep. Coincidentally, many of the old brick ovens were falling into disrepair and were thus abandoned or covered up. abandoned or covered up.

The story of today's factory-produced bread is very different. Baking methods may have improved, but what of the quality of the bread? The constant demand for loaves baked in the old brick-oven of Derwen Bakery is answer enough. There is *no* baking like the old baking!

Recipes for Home Baking

BARA GWYN — WHITE BREAD

3½ lbs plain flour	1.5kg
3 teaspoons salt	3 × 5ml spoon
4 teaspoons sugar	4 × 5ml spoon
1½ pints warm water	900ml
1 oz yeast	30g

Place the flour and salt in a warm bowl. Cream the yeast and sugar and pour into a well in the centre of the flour. Cover the yeast mixture with a little of the flour, and leave in a warm place until it becomes frothy. Then proceed to mix the dough, adding the warm water gradually. Knead well for about 10 minutes until the hands and sides of the bowl are free of dough. Cover the bowl and leave in a warm place until the dough has doubled its original size. Then turn it out on to a floured board, divide and mould into loaves according to the size of the tins. Place each loaf into a warm greased tin and leave to rise again for another half hour. Then bake in a moderately hot oven (400°F, 200°C, Gas 5) for approximately 1½ hours, according to size.

BARA GWENITH — WHEAT BREAD

2 lbs wholemeal flour	1kg
¾ oz dried yeast	25g
A little sugar	
Pinch of salt	
A knob of butter (optional)	
1 pint warm water	600ml

Place the flour and salt in a warm bowl and rub the butter into it. Cream the sugar and yeast until moist and blend with a little warm water. Pour the yeast mixture into a well in the centre of the dry ingredients, cover it with a little flour and leave to stand in a warm place for 20-30 minutes. Then knead into a soft dough, using the remainder of the water as required. Return the bowl to a warm place and allow the dough to rise for 1 hour. Then turn it out on to a floured board and knead quickly for 2 minutes. Divide the dough into 2 equal parts, place in greased, warm tins and allow to rise for another ½ hour. Then bake the loaves in a hot oven (400°F, 200°C, Gas 5) for approximately 1 hour, according to size.

BARA BRITH — CURRANT BREAD

2 lbs plain flour	1kg
1 oz yeast	30g
12 oz butter	360g
6 oz soft brown sugar	180g
6 oz currants	180g
6 oz sultanas	180g
3 oz raisins	90g
2 oz candied peel	60g
¼ teaspoon nutmeg or mixed spice	½ × 2.5ml spoon
½ teaspoon salt	1 × 2.5ml spoon
2 eggs	
1 tablespoon black treacle	1 × 15ml spoon
a little warm milk and warm water	

Place the flour in a mixing bowl and allow to stand in a warm place for a short while. Rub in the butter, add all the other dry ingredients and mix thoroughly. Cream the yeast with a little sugar and blend it with half a cupful of warm milk. Make a well in the centre of the dry ingredients, pour in the yeast mixture and sprinkle with a little flour. Cover and allow to stand in a warm place for a few minutes. Beat the eggs, pour on the yeast mixture and proceed to knead into a soft dough. Melt the treacle in a little warm water and gradually add it to the dough, as required, when kneading. Cover the bowl and allow the dough to rise for 1½ hours in a warm place. Turn out on to a well-floured board, divide into equal parts and place in warm greased tins. Bake the loaves in a moderately hot oven (375°F, 190°C, Gas 5) for 1-1½ hours.

BARA CRAI — UNLEAVENED BREAD

1 lb plain, white flour	*480g*
½ teaspoon salt	*1 × 2.5ml spoon*
½ teaspoon bicarbonate of soda	*1 × 2.5ml spoon*
½ pint buttermilk	*300ml*
a few currants (optional)	

Place the flour in a bowl and work in the salt and currants. Dissolve the soda in the warm buttermilk and pour gradually into the flour. Mix all together to make a soft dough. Knead lightly and turn out on to a floured board. Shape the dough into a round flat loaf, rolling it lightly with a rolling pin. Place the loaf on a greased, hot bakestone or heavy frying pan and bake until the surface begins to harden. Turn and bake on the other side.

This unleavened bread was commonly prepared as a stop gap when the week's supply of bread fell short before the regular baking day. The ingredients varied slightly, according to local custom — water was used as an alternative to buttermilk for mixing it, and sugar and currants were optional extras in some areas.

BARA CEIRCH — OATCAKES

1 tablespoon luke-warm water	*1 × 15ml spoon*
½ teaspoon bacon dripping	*1 × 2.5ml spoon*
3 oz oatmeal	*90g*

Melt the dripping in the water and then gradually add the oatmeal, kneading the mixture to a soft dough. Turn out on to a wooden board sprinkled with a little oatmeal and mould the dough between the two hands to form a small cone. Flatten the cone with the palm of the hand to form a small round cake. Keeping this basic shape, proceed to roll out with a rolling pin. To ensure even rolling, give the cake an occasional quarter turn, paying particular attention to the fine edge. Roll out to form a large thin oatcake, approximately 10″ in diameter. Place the oatcake on a moderately hot griddle or bakestone and bake on both sides until it acquires a light golden colour. Finally, allow it to harden in a warm place before storing.

Acknowledgements

This booklet could not have been written without the kind co-operation of many persons. The text is greatly enriched with oral information gathered widely from Welsh housewives and bakers. Excerpts from recorded interviews punctuate most sections; these were edited and translated by my colleague, Mrs. Beth Thomas. I am indebted to her for fulfilling this arduous and painstaking task. The original tapes are kept in the Welsh Folk Museum sound archive.

I wish to thank the following individuals for information and the loan of family photographs:

Miss C. Davies, Tonyrefail, Mid Glamorgan
Mrs. C. Evans, Cynllwyd, Gwynedd
Mrs. E. Evans, Blaenau Ffestiniog, Gwynedd
Mrs. E.M. Hughes, Llannerch-y-medd, Gwynedd
D. Hinton Jones, Aberystwyth, Dyfed
D.E. Lloyd Jones, London
Mrs. M. Jones, Llanrwst, Clwyd
Mrs. L. Davies-Jones, Menai Bridge, Gwynedd
Mrs. A. Mainwaring, Port Talbot, West Glamorgan
P.J. Moore, Aberystwyth, Dyfed
A. Price, Aberffraw, Gwynedd
Mrs. E. Roberts, Bryncroes, Gwynedd
Mrs. E. Rogers, Ffair Rhos, Dyfed
Mrs. A. Rosser, Llansamlet, West Glamorgan
Miss J.C. Williams, Rhosbeirio.

Photographs of the present day Derwen Bakery were taken by Mr. Michael Isaac with the kind co-operation of Mrs. Chris Aston, and it is my privilege to thank her and her staff for 'keeping the fires burning' and so successfully reviving one of the oldest of domestic skills.

Further Reading

C. Anne Wilson, *Food and Drink in Britain*, London, 1973.

Elizabeth David, *English Bread and Yeast Cookery*, London, 1977.

R. Sheppard and Edward Newtown, *The Story of Bread*, London, 1957.

William Cobbett, *Cottage Economy*, Oxford, 1979, pp. 48-71.

Eurwyn Wiliam, 'Yr Aelwyd: the architectural development of the hearth in Wales' in *Folk Life* volume 16, 1978, pp. 85-100.